Let's Form a Band!

Haydn Middleton
Character illustrations by Jonatronix

Contents

All kinds of bands

It can be fun to play a musical instrument. It can be even better to team up with other **musicians** to play in a band. There are many different types of band:

What types of bands are these?

1

2

3

I love this band – they rock!

Answers on p24

Making a great sound

There are all sorts of instruments. They all make different sounds. By playing different instruments together at the same time you can make even more sounds.

The band *The Feeling* on stage.

Each person in a band has a vital job to do. Bit by bit they build up the sound for a song. Some people sing as well as play an instrument.

Sometimes one musician within a band will play a **solo**. This gives the musician a chance to show off how well he can play his own instrument. The other members of the band can have a rest!

The *Jimi Hendrix Experience*, 1970. Jimi Hendrix was famous for his guitar solos.

Destiny's Child, 2002.

Some bands, like *Destiny's Child*, are vocal groups. Their voices work in harmony to make a fantastic sound. They don't play instruments but they do have backing music. This adds extra layers of sound to the songs they perform.

Songwriting teams

All bands need good songs and tunes to play. Some bands play other people's songs. Most bands like to write their own songs. John Lennon and Paul McCartney of *The Beatles* were one of the world's most famous songwriting teams.

These are just some of the famous songs that Lennon and McCartney wrote together:

- A Hard Day's Night
- With A Little Help From My Friends
- I Want To Hold Your Hand
- From Me To You
- Let It Be
- She Loves You

Paul McCartney (left) and John Lennon (right) – the songwriters in *The Beatles*.

Danger Mouse (left) used **samples** of Beatles' songs on an early record. Then he teamed up to write new songs with Cee-Lo Green (right). They formed the band *Gnarls Barkley*.

Gnarls Barkley at the MTV Music Awards, 2006.

They worked very well together. The first single they ever released was called 'Crazy'. It was so successful that it went to the top of the UK singles chart. They went on to win several awards.

Getting heard

All bands love to play their music for other people to hear. This means that bands have to travel around playing **gigs**. Hopefully the people at the gig will like the band and tell their friends.

Rich and famous bands travel around in luxury. Some even have their own private jets. But being in a band is not always glamorous!

The *Rolling Stones* are a famous rock band. They first started playing gigs in 1962 and are still playing today.

They've been playing together for ... nearly 50 years. Amazing!

Mick Jagger (centre, vocals) and Keith Richards (centre-left, guitar) have been in the band since it started.

The Rolling Stones: Fact file

Formed: 1962

Current line up: Mick Jagger (vocals), Keith Richards (guitar), Ronnie Wood (bass guitar) and Charlie Watts (drums)

Achievements:
32 UK & US Top 10 singles
43 UK & US Top 10 albums
Over 200 million albums sold worldwide
Highest earning music tour ever – summer 2007

Help from the Internet

There are other ways to get your band heard. Many bands record songs on to a computer and put them on an Internet site like MySpace or YouTube. Other people can log on and listen in. Then they can tell their friends how great you are!

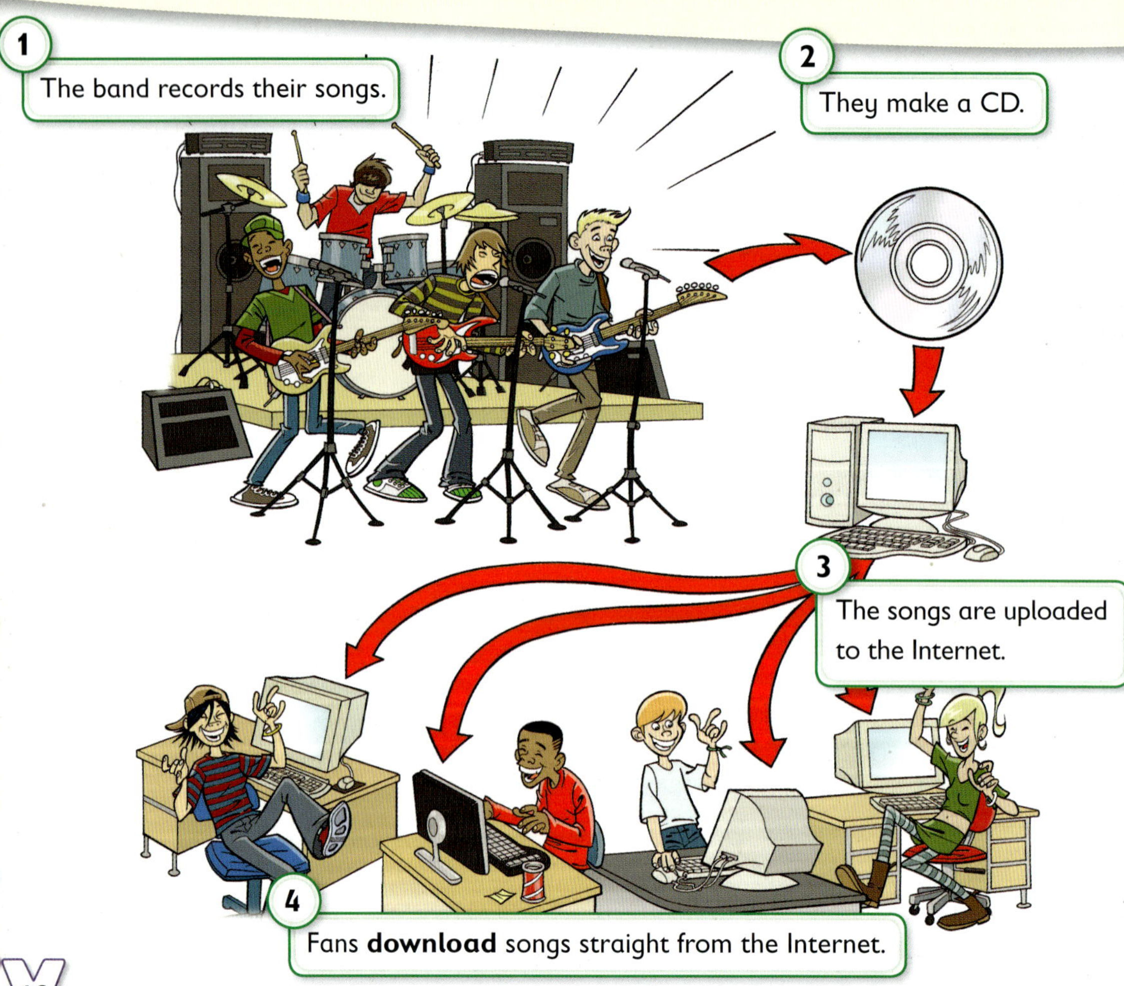

The *Arctic Monkeys* gave away home-made CDs at their first gigs. Fans put this music on their computers and then shared it with their friends. That way, the band were famous before a record company had even signed them.

From free CDs to fame and fortune – the *Arctic Monkeys* live on stage in 2007.

Getting together

Many bands are formed by friends who enjoy playing music together.

Arashi – a Japanese boy band formed by a record company.

Girls Aloud – a British girl band who won a talent show.

Sometimes a record company wants a particular type of band, so they will **audition** for members. Sometimes judges on TV talent shows pick who should be in a band.

One band, *Gorillaz*, doesn't even have people in it. It is a band of cartoon characters (but with real musicians who write and make the music).

The *Gorrillaz* – a cartoon band.

The whole of *Band Aid* singing together in the recording studio, 1984.

Bob Geldof in Africa.

Some bands get together for just one record or gig. Usually it's for charity. In 1984 the musicians Bob Geldof and Midge Ure formed *Band Aid*. This band recorded only one single – 'Do They Know It's Christmas?'

The song was a massive hit. *Band Aid* raised lots of money to help famine victims in Africa.

In 2004 another version of the song was recorded for charity.

There are lots of people who help out a band. They are a really important part of the team. These might include:

- a record company that produces the music
- a manager who sorts out the money
- a person who books the gigs
- a sound engineer who makes sure all the equipment works and that the band sounds the way it's supposed to
- roadies who transport and set up all the stage equipment
- wardrobe, hair and make-up artists who help the band look good on stage
- a **choreographer** who might help teach the band to dance.

A roadie setting up the equipment ready for a gig.

Going solo

Some band members get tired of being in a team. They can't agree on what sort of music to play any more. So they leave and go solo instead.

Take That in 2007 ... without Robbie Williams!

Take That was a hit band that split up. But, not every member had a successful solo career. Nine years after the band split, they got back together. All except for one member – Robbie Williams. He was very successful on his own, so he stayed solo.

Robbie Williams continues to be a successful solo musician.

Team colours

Members of sports teams wear matching kits. The players in some bands wear matching clothes, too. It helps them feel part of a team. Would *you* want to look like any of these bands?

Wow! They must get so hot in those suits.

Wombles

Coldplay

A band is born

Micro-Band fact-file

Lead guitar: Max

Vocals and bass guitar: Cat

Keyboard: Ant

Drums: Tiger

People we need to hire: manager, sound engineer, roadies

First gig: when we've written some songs together

Musical heroes: Rolling Stones, Destiny's Child, Arctic Monkeys, Robbie Williams (Cat only!)

Ambition: to play together forever!

Glossary

audition	an interview for a musician where a person has to prove they can play an instrument or sing
choreographer	a person who makes up dance steps and teaches other people how to do them
download	copying information from the Internet to your computer
gigs	performances or concerts by a band
harmony	musical notes mixed together
musicians	people who play musical instruments
rhythm	the patterns made in music by weak and strong sounds
samples	bits of music you take off one record to use to make another one
solo	something sung, played, danced or done by one person
vocals	musical performance with singing

Answers

1. Brass
2. Jazz
3. Steel
4. School
5. Pop
6. Rock